Libra Sun, And The Moons That Follow

Poetry on Love, Loss, and the Light That Remains

Jaynell Falk

BookLeaf Publishing

India | USA | UK

Made with ❤ on the BookLeaf Publishing Platform
www.bookleafpub.in
www.bookleafpub.com

Dedication

To the ones who carry the weight of love in their bones, who have known the quiet ache of absence, who have whispered their longing to the stars and found their own echoes in the moonlight.

To the ones who have stayed soft despite the breaking, who have learned to hold both fire and tenderness without losing themselves to either.

To the ones who have loved, lost, and still dare to open their hands to the sky—

This is for you.

Preface

*"Some nights the sky wept stars that it would never see
again, and in that moment, I understood that I was the
sky."*

—*Pavana Reddy*

———

There is something timeless about the way we love.
Something vast, like the night sky, like the tide
stretching toward the moon even as it retreats. Love is
both presence and absence, the light and the longing, the
moment we arrive and the space we leave behind.

I have spent my life trying to balance the weight of both.
Trying to find stillness between the pull of passion and
the quiet of solitude. Trying to understand why some
love stays like constellations—fixed and unwavering—
while others burn out before we can name them.

This collection is born from that search. These poems are
the echoes of love that lingers, the shadows of goodbyes
that never quite leave us, the light we carry even when
we think we are empty.

You may find yourself in these words. You may see the
reflection of someone you once knew, someone you once

were. Or perhaps, like me, you are still learning that love
—real love—is not always about holding on, but about
learning to shine even after the dark.

No matter where you are in your journey, know this:

You are light.
You are seen.
You remain.

-Jaynell Falk

Acknowledgements

To the love that shaped me—thank you for teaching me the language of longing, the poetry of presence, the lessons that linger even in silence.

To my ancestors, who walked before me and wrote their stories in my blood—your wisdom hums in my heartbeat. Your strength carries me forward.

To my family, my foundation, my forever—your love is the gravity that holds me steady.

To my dearest friends, the ones who have held space for my light and my shadow—you are the constellations that guide me home.

To the heartbreaks that became poetry, the losses that became lessons, the nights that turned to pages—thank you for giving me something to write about.

And to you, the reader, who has found yourself in these words—thank you for letting my voice live in your world, even if just for a moment.

This book is ours.

With love,
Jaynell Falk

Born Under a Libra Sun

I have spent my life
trying to fold myself into the calm,
into polite,
into don't rock the boat
just because you know how to swim.

I was steady.
I was soft.
I was what they called
"Easy to love"—
as long as I kept the fire
on low.

I was born with flames in my fists.
A hunger in my bones
for something that bites back.
For something louder
than survival.

I am both storm
and shelter,
both gospel
and scream.

and I will not
cut myself in half
to fit your version of whole.

The Moons That Follow

People don't leave—
some echo.
They bleed through the seams
of your silence,
dripping into places
you thought were healed.

Showing up in songs you skip,
in the midnight breath you hold
without meaning to.

And they loved you,
like the ocean—
receding from shores
never staying long enough
to drown you fully,
but just enough to keep you soaked.

And now?
even after the sky has emptied itself
of their glow,
The night doesn't hit like it used to.
It's softer.

Still bruised,
but softer.

Because even absence
has fingerprints,
and they left theirs on your tide.

The Way Love Leaves

It doesn't pack bags.
It forgets things.
A mug half-full by the sink.
Your voice reverberating off spaces
that used to feel warm.

In the way colors drain from old film—
gradually,
unannounced.

In the smell of their shampoo
on a pillow you never touch anymore.
In jokes you no longer tell
because they never laughed
the way you needed them to.
In the distance between goodbyes
of people that no longer speak.

A gentle fading,
until there is nothing left to cross.

And one day,
you're standing

in a room you both built,
wondering
when it stopped
being yours.

The Girl Who Loved
the Moon Too Much

I have always reached for things
that were too far away.
Stars, love,
people who never knew how to stay.

The moon was my first heartbreak.
Always there, but never mine.
Always glowing,
but slipping through the sky
before I could call it home.

The Moon Never Chose
the Tide, Either

I did not ask for this pull,
this yearning for something
that is always moving away.

I did not choose to love
as the tide loves the moon—
restless, rising, reaching,
only to be left in waves.

But even knowing,
I still move toward you,
as if longing alone
could rewrite the sky.

In the Light That Remains

I have gaps in my childhood
where love should have lived.
Places where lullabies
were swallowed by silence,
where I learned to mother myself
long before I understood
what that meant.

But time, in its strange mercy,
gave us back to each other—
not in the way I had dreamed,
but in the only way we knew how.

The years softened us.
Pain once laced with thunder
became quiet confessions.
And in the last stretch of borrowed time,
you reached for me,
and I let you in.

Now, I see you in the mirror,
in the way my hands move through the world,
in the small ways I have become you.

I used to wonder what it would feel like
to truly be yours.
Now, I know.

Even if only in the light
that remains.

A Constellation of Ghosts

There are of bodies of stars housed within,
where the dead still walk.
Each one answers to the names
of the ones I've lost.

My mother
still walks barefoot
through the kitchen
of my memory,
singing that song—
the one I never learned
but somehow still hear
on cloudy days.

My father
still a shadow
leaning against the doorway,
shaped like an unfinished sentence.
Carved out of
everything he didn't say.

They live here,
inside the house of my body.

Not because I'm haunted—
I made a home for them.
Where else would they go?
Who else could love them in the way I
still do?

Grief is just love
with nowhere else to go.

And maybe
I haven't let them go
because they never really left.

They just changed rooms.

Moonlight Kisses

There are some kisses
you will never feel.
Hands you will never hold.
Loves you will only know
through the distance between you.

And still,
you will love them.
And still,
they will change you.

Wish Amongst the Skies

I planted my dreams,
left them to sprout between heartbeats,
unrushed,
unseen by the world that would not understand.

I am the sky at dusk—
holding shadows tight,
unafraid of the stars I've yet to become,
and the moonlight still hesitant to touch me.

No voices of hope
but the weight of the wind that carries it.
Not the spark that ignites,
but the embers that twinkle
long after the fire has burned out.

There is no map for this journey,
no call to arms,
no loud declaration of arrival.
I simply move
in the direction of my own pulse,
my own rhythm.

I no longer seek permission
from the clouds or the stars.
I am the pulse between them,
the breath of something undefined,
reaching for the sky without asking to be seen.

My wish has never been to be found.
It has always been to find the places within me
that are enough to stand in their own light.

Laughter: A Rebellion Against the Dark, Stardust Scattered Across Time

You laughed
even when things were ending,
and that mattered.

Not because it fixed anything
but because
you did it anyway.

Let joy be a rebellion,
as if we are defying the universe.
Let your laughter roll like thunder
against everything that ever
tried to break you—
as if daring it
to take our joy,
only to watch us
create more.

Laughter is proof

that we were here.
That we burned,
that we shimmered,
that we refused
to be forgotten.

Somewhere in those black,
velvet skies,
a star is born every time
you refuse to let sadness
swallow you whole.

The Light We Carry

There was only breath,
ghost-thin,
threaded between the
grief of your short presence, and
what couldn't be said.

My fingers
folded into memories
like a child
reaching backward
through time—
not to comfort, just to stay.

hands
still warm—
but drifting.
A softness left behind
like perfume on old silk,
barely clinging,
barely there.

I gave your name to the river—
written on trembling paper,

a lantern in my hands
that held more truth than
any eulogy could.

Carved my farewells into
water, spoken only
to the dusk, and sealed
by the weight of
absence that settled quietly
inside the softest part of me.

I lit it,
drew roses along its skin.
Let the wind drag my tears
like it knew how to hold sorrow
without ceremony.

This is the light we carry—
not brilliance, but endurance.
Its tender and private.
It flickers in the ruin
and still makes room for warmth.

The kind
you take home
without asking why.
because if you do—

you might break.

It lives there
long after the world forgets
who left you.

Laced in Starlight

Some souls are tied together
by more than just time,
by more than just circumstance.
You are mine.

We have walked separate roads,
chased different dreams,
loved and lost and become
in ways we never imagined,
and still—
we are here.

You are the one who sees me
in every form I take,
who holds space for my joys and my sorrows,
who knows my history
not as a story I tell,
but as something you have lived beside me.

Some friendships are fleeting,
measured in seasons.
Ours is infinite,
woven in the fabric of the years,

laced in starlight,
written into the sky itself.

No need for a compass
when the constellations spell your name.
No need for words
when love already knows
exactly where to find us.

If Love Had a Sound

It wouldn't be loud.
It wouldn't beg for attention.
It would sit in a room with its back turned
and hope you notice it breathing.

It might sound like
a single glass
set down too gently.
like fingers brushing skin
and that used to know it.
Like the word *stay*
caught in someone's throat.

If love had a sound,
it'd be the quite
after you said
you were okay
and I didn't believe you.

It'd be a song
half-remembered
until it played
midway through a breakdown

on the highway,
windows down,
no one there to turn it off.

It would sound like dusk
leaning into your collarbone.
Like someone kissing you
just to memorize
how your soul exhales.
In the pause
after someone says
"I miss you"
and means it.

And maybe—
maybe it's nothing.
Just
you,
alone,
listening for something
that doesn't make noise anymore.

When the Moon Asked for My Name

I spoke it in a whisper,
as if I had only just remembered.
Somewhere between night and dawn,
that strange middle space
where you stop looking for peace
and start holding your own pieces.
I became something else entirely.

We Love Like the Stars Breaking

Love can arrive slow,
soft, steady—
lingering like
a candle burning low.

Ours was louder.

A collapse of galaxies,
a fire streaking through the sky,
too bright,
too wild,
too quick to last.

But oh my,
doesn't it make the night
beautiful while it burns?

Sonata: To the Moon & Stars

There are loves that hum in the night,
Soft as moonbeams tracing silent air,
They pulse beneath the stars, out of our sight,
A song composed of moments unaware.

Your name, a constellation etched in time,
Unspoken, yet it stirs the space I breathe,
A warmth that stretches far, but stays in love,
A melody I hear, though it's not in my sight.

I watch you from the constellations near,
Two souls aligned, yet worlds apart in sound,
A symphony of longing, never late,
A harmony that persists, nevermore found.

Had fate been kinder, we might have known more,
But here, in silence, we learn what we adore.

The Morning After Forever

We said forever in the hush of midnight,
believed in it like something holy,
like something the world could never break.

But forever is fragile.
It shatters in the morning light,
dissolves in the void between breaths.

I do not regret loving you,
only that love isn't always enough.

Mars & the Gravity Between Us

Some friendships arrive like a spark—
quick and bright, burning briefly before the dark.

Ours, however, was never that.
It was the pull of something steady,
a quiet knowing in the space between us,
like tugging tides,
like gravity itself—
constant,
holding us together even when unseen.

We have carried one another
through the weight of storms unasked for,
holding space for grief
without letting it define us.

We've laughed in defiance
when the world tried to steal our joy,
each giggle a rebellion
against the weight of loss.

Brother—not by blood,
but by every unspoken promise,
every story passed between the hours,
every moment whispered—
you are not alone.

This is what we are—
a bond that does not bend,
a love that requires no proof,
a force as unwavering as the stars.

Some people drift and fade
into the shadows of time,
but there are those who remain,
who tether you to light
when the world is too dark.

We are that kind,
rooted in quiet understanding.
And I am forever grateful
to the universe for giving me you.

When the Stars Spoke Us Into Being

You knew my mother before me—
her laughter blazed through your childhood,
her voice lingered in rooms you once called
home.

Yet, when I entered your world,
I was no stranger,
only a name already written in the stars,
a thread woven before time touched our hands.

We were young,
wild as meteor showers,
too small to grasp the weight of love,
yet it pulled us near.

Through years of shedding selves,
of vast and endless becoming,
you remained—
never dimming my fire,
never fearing the light I would grow into.

And when the world said love was fragile,
that it would burn out if tested,
you proved them wrong.

You loved me through every revolution,
every eclipse, every collision,
through the long journey home
to my own sky.

You are my love—
not by fate's decree,
but because across galaxies, across lifetimes,
we would have found and chosen each other,
again and again.

Ode to My Cosmic Body

Once, I cursed this celestial skin—
the soft terrain of stretch and curve,
this Venus-forged form.

I traced the abyss,
aching to be something smaller,
something untouched by time and gravity.

But now I honor the orbits of my hips,
the star trails along my thighs,
the molten glow of Venus at my core,

and whisper to the universe within me:
*"You are the atoms of stars—
the cosmos made flesh."*

The Anatomy of Scales

I am the weight of the world in my hands—
a scale with no resting place.
Not built to lean
but always swaying
where chaos
brushes shoulder with calm.

I hold the sun in one hand,
the moon in the other—
each pulling me
in quiet opposition,
and yet I remain.

I am the space between upheavals,
in the breath
that doesn't choose a side.
measuring every shift—
the cost of standing unmoved,
the ache of motion.

The world tips
and I do not chase balance
as if it is a prize.

I only ask:
how softly
can I hold contradiction
without breaking?

I am the Libra—
a living fulcrum
always adjusting,
always holding,
always asking,
if harmony is a truth
we stumble upon
or just a burden
we learn
to bear.

www.ingramcontent.com/pod-product-compliance
Lightning Source LLC
La Vergne TN
LVHW021312200726
843509LV00012B/1876

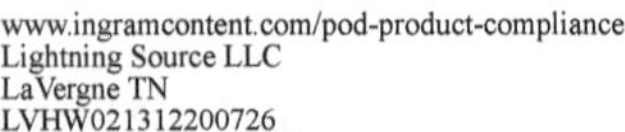